THE MAKING OF

The Wind in the Willows

THE MAKING OF

The Wind in the Willows

PETER HUNT

Bodleian Library
UNIVERSITY OF OXFORD

First published in 2018 by the Bodleian Library
Broad Street, Oxford OX1 3BG

www.bodleianshop.co.uk

ISBN: 978 1 85124 479 9

Text © Peter Hunt, 2018

All images, unless specified on pp. 110–11 © Bodleian Library, University of Oxford, 2018.

Peter Hunt has asserted his right to be identified as the author of this Work.

Cover design by Dot Little at the Bodleian Library
Designed and typeset by Laura Parker in 9.4 pt on 16.4 pt Fedra Serif Pro
Printed and bound by Great Wall Printing Co. Ltd, Hong Kong, on 157 gsm Gold East paper

British Library Catalogue in Publishing Data
A CIP record of this publication is available from the British Library

CONTENTS

1

THE MYSTERIES OF
THE WIND IN THE WILLOWS

The Wind in the Willows is one of the most famous English children's books, one of the most famous books about animals and a classic book about 'messing about in boats'.

Famous, it certainly is. Although it has never been quite the international icon that *Alice's Adventures in Wonderland* has become, Kenneth Grahame's eccentric masterpiece can be read in Afrikaans as *Die Wind in die Wilgers*, in Italian as *Il Vento nei Salici*, in Finnish as *Kaislikossa suhisee*, in Portuguese as *As Aventuras de Senhor Sapo* and in dozens of other languages. It is currently available in well over fifty

Kenneth Grahame at thirty: a rising young banker, and at the same time one of 'W.E. Henley's Young Men', writing short essays for the *Scots Observer*.

editions in English: there are versions in verse, graded readers for learning English as a foreign language, audio and video adaptations, plays (notably by A.A. Milne and Alan Bennett), films, picture books (with or without stickers), pop-up books, knitting patterns, graphic novels and scholarly annotated editions. There are sequels, such as William Horwood's *The Willows in Winter* (1993), gospel meditations, a cookery book and Robert de Board's *Counselling for Toads* (1998), an introduction to psychotherapy. E.H. Shepard's illustrations have been used on national postage stamps and to advertise England itself in the 1980s English Tourist Board series, 'Making a Break for the Real England'. The book has been the inspiration for a sculpture trail, one of the most successful rides in Disneyland and a musical adaptation (by Julian Fellowes) in 2016, which was the first London West End musical to raise £1 million through crowdfunding.

What makes all this mysterious (apart from the fact that this quintessentially English book was written by a Scot) is that *The Wind in the Willows* is not a children's book at all – neither the author nor the original publishers ever suggested that it was. Nor is it an animal story: the characters are, as one of the original reviewers, the novelist Arnold Bennett, observed, 'meant to be nothing but human beings', or as Margaret Blount in her book on animals in fiction, *Animal Land*, put it, 'for animals, read chaps'.[1] And boats appear substantially in only two of the twelve chapters. Even the title is mysterious – the word 'willows' never appears in the book: Grahame's original suggestion for a title was *Mr Mole and his Mates*.

But, surely, it is a book about small and not so small animals – a Toad, a Rat, a Mole and a Badger (and therefore this *must* be a children's book). If so, then these are animals who drink and smoke, own houses,

drive (and steal) cars, row boats, escape from jail, yearn for gastronomic nights in Italy, eat ham and eggs for breakfast and write poetry – while Toad combs his hair, and the Mole has a black velvet smoking-jacket.

Of course, *very* occasionally they behave like animals. Mr Mole, in the midst of thoroughly human spring-cleaning, briefly turns into a mole, scrabbling and scrooging his way to the surface; the aristocratic Otter, languidly enjoying a riverbank picnic (which includes cold tongue, pickled gherkins and lemonade) suddenly turns into an otter and swallows a passing mayfly.

Nor are we always sure how large these characters are – Grahame plays virtuoso tricks with scale. In the chapter 'Wayfarer's All', the Water Rat, a country poet of independent means, strolls discontentedly on the Downs before plunging into a wheat field where, suddenly, the 'stiff strong stalks … carried their own golden sky away over his head' and he gets into conversation with field-mice who are preparing for the winter by examining 'plans and drawings of small flats, stated to be desirable and compact, and situated conveniently near the stores.'[2] Most spectacular of these shifts – dizzying in its play with scale and perspective, as well as with class and character – is Toad's encounter with the barge-woman.

Mr Toad, at this point in the story, has absconded from his country house, stolen a car and escaped from jail disguised as a washerwoman. He finds himself on a canal narrowboat, coerced into actually doing some washing, which the barge-woman finds highly amusing.

> Toad's temper, which had been simmering viciously for some time, now fairly boiled over, and he lost all control of himself.

The all-male riverside idyll: E.H. Shepard's vision of *The Wind in the Willows*.

'You common, low, *fat* barge-woman!' he shouted; 'don't you dare to talk to your betters like that! Washerwoman indeed! I would have you know that I am a Toad, a very well-known respected, distinguished Toad! I may be under a bit of a cloud at present, but I will *not* be laughed at by a barge-woman!'

The woman moved nearer to him and peered under his bonnet keenly and closely. 'Why, so you are!' she cried. 'Well, I never! A horrid, nasty, crawly Toad! And in my nice clean barge, too! Now that I will *not* have.' ... One big mottled arm shot out and caught Toad by a fore-leg, while the other gripped him fast by a hind-leg ... and Toad found himself flying through the air, revolving rapidly as he went.[3]

This is mischievous stuff, appealing to the mischievous in its readers, and children may well be less inhibited in accepting it than adults.

But such sleights of hand are very rare, and for the most part, the book is about a group of well-off, leisured English gentlemen. Even more importantly, the book hardly ever addresses itself to an audience of children: as Humphrey Carpenter put it, '*The Wind in the Willows* has nothing to do with childhood or children, except that it can be enjoyed by the young.'[4]

Of course, it begins – and began – as a children's book. Like other famous children's books – such as *Alice's Adventures in Wonderland*,

OPPOSITE 'There's cold chicken ... coldtonguecoldhamcoldbeefpickledgherkinssalad-frenchrollscresssandwidgespottedmeatgingerbeerlemonadesodawater—' Arthur Rackham's 1939 view of the iconic picnic.

OVERLEAF An affectionate letter from father to son, written from Fowey in the summer of 1907, in which we meet the first version of the barge-woman.

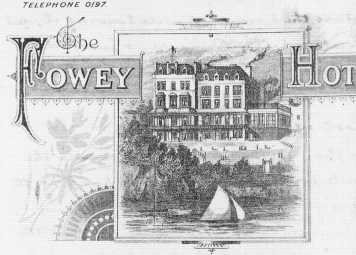

FOWEY, CORNWALL, 7th June 1907.

My dearest Mouse

I hope you are having better
weather than we are getting here. It is so w
& windy here that we cannot go out rowing in
boats, or fly kites, or sail, or anything.

You may be wishing to hear what
further things happened to Toad on his wa
home, after his escape from the policemen wh
were pursuing him to take him back to pri
Well, next morning the sun shone brightly in
the hollow tree, & woke up Mr. Toad, who was
sleeping soundly after his fatiguing exertion
of the previous day. He got up, shook hims
combed the dead leaves out of his hair wit
his fingers, & set off walking briskly, for he

ry cold & rather hungry. Well. he walked & he walked,
& he came to a canal, & he thought that must lead
to a town, so he walked along the tow-path, &
presently he met a horse, with a long rope attached
to it, towing a barge; & he waited for the barge
to come up, & there was a man steering it, & he
nodded, & said "Goodmorning, washerwoman!
what are you doing here?" Then the toad made
a pitifull face, & said "Please, kind Sir, I am
going to pay a visit to my married daughter,
who lives near a fine house called 'Toad Hall';
but I've lost my way, & spent all my money, &
im very tired". Then the man said "Toad Hall?
Why, I'm going that way myself. Jump in,
& I'll give you a lift". So he steered the barge
close to the bank, & the toad stepped on
board & sat down, very pleased with himself.
Presently the man said "I don't see why I should
give you a lift for nothing, so you take that
tub of water standing over there, & that bit of
yellow soap, & here are some shirts, & you can
be washing them as we go along". Then the toad
was rather frightened, for he had never washed
a shirt in his life; but he dabbed the shirt into
the water, & he dabbed some soap on it, but
it never seemed to get any cleaner, & his
fingers got very cold & he began to get
very cross. Presently the man came to
see how he was getting on, & burst out
laughing at him, & said "Call yourself a
washerwoman? That's not the way to wash

The Hobbit and *Treasure Island* – it started life as a story for a particular child, and this shows most in the opening chapter. Like all these books, *The Wind in the Willows* grew in the writing and ended up as something quite different from, and something much more complex than, a bedtime story. But whereas *Alice's Adventures* is a children's book that can be read by adults, *The Wind in the Willows* is an adult's book that can be read by children. This is because (and this also accounts for its relative lack of international success) its landscapes and cultural references are deeply embedded in Edwardian England – whereas Alice moves in a detached world of fantasy, and the many period references in that book are hidden in the background.

Even more disconcerting for readers trying to pigeon-hole *The Wind in the Willows* is its structure – and the mystery of how it does not collapse. It can be read as two separate and contrasting stories – one about Mole's acceptance into a conservative, elitist society, the other about Toad's rebellious rejection of it. These two stories are carefully balanced – both Mole and Toad reach their nadirs in hollow trees – and the whole book is structured as a classical epic, with Toad, in the chapter 'The Return of Ulysses', having a suitably ragged Homeric homecoming.

But this is only half the problem with this structural enigma of a book: into which genre does it fit? The answer to that is that Grahame ruthlessly borrowed from and played with the major popular genres of his day: the river book, the caravanning book, the motoring thriller, the rural idyll (complete with Christmas carol), the pseudo-mystic 'spiritual' writing of the 'decadents' (complete with miasmic pagan verse) and, of course, the rollicking boys' adventure story. And he cheerfully parodies George Borrow, W.S. Gilbert and Sherlock Holmes, caricatures his friends and celebrates his own delights and frustrations.

1 The River Bank

The Mole had been working very hard all the morning, spring-cleaning his little home. First with brooms, then with dusters; then on ladders and steps and chairs, with a brush and a pail of whitewash; till he had dust in his throat + eyes, + splashes of whitewash all over his black fur, + an aching back + weary arms. Spring was moving in the air above + in the earth below + around him, penetrating even his dark + lowly little house with its spirit of divine discontent + longing. It was small wonder, then, that he suddenly flung down his brush on the floor, said "Bother!" and "O blow!" and also "Hang spring-cleaning!" and bolted out of the house without even waiting to put on his coat. Something up above was calling him imperiously, and he made for the steep little tunnel which answered in his case to the gravelled carriage-drive owned by animals whose residences are nearer to the sun + air. So he scraped + scratched and scrabbled + scrooged, and then he scrooged again + scrabbled

The beginning of revolt: the manuscript of Chapter I of The Wind in the Willows, *from the Bodleian Library.*

One of the mystifying things for those who would try to make *The Wind in the Willows* into a children's book is its attitude to adventure. Anything likely to disturb its cosy world is ruthlessly suppressed – the Mole stops the Rat from heading to the warm south in 'Wayfarers All'; Toad's rebellion is crushed by all his 'friends' – and the Mole's initial, childlike curiosity about the world is put firmly in its place in the very first chapter. As he and Rat row along the peaceful river, the Mole looks into the distance:

> 'And beyond the Wild Wood again?' he asked; 'where it's all blue and dim, and one sees what may be hills or perhaps they mayn't, and something like the smoke of towns, or is it only cloud-drift?'
>
> 'Beyond the Wild Wood comes the Wide World,' said the Rat. 'And that's something that doesn't matter, either to you or me. I've never been there, and I'm never going, nor you either, if you've got any sense at all. Don't ever refer to it again, please. Now then! Here's our backwater at last, where we're going to lunch.'[5]

This certainly concurs with the romantic idea that children's books should be safe, and the Edwardian period has been portrayed – especially in children's literature – as peaceful and retreatist. In fact, it was a period of political and cultural instability, change and fear. Rumours of war – especially, although not exclusively, with Germany – were common; the German battle-fleet was expanding; the Boer wars had shaken Britain's faith in its army. No wonder the Water Rat is

The luxurious interior of Gordon Stables' 'land yacht', complete with *everything*. From G. Stables, *The Cruise of the Land Yacht 'Wanderer'*, 1886.

no fan of the Wide World. Things were worse closer to home. In 1903 the Women's Social and Political Union was founded by Emmeline Pankhurst, and the speed limit for motor cars was increased to 20 mph (32 km/h); in 1906 the Labour Representation Committee won twenty-nine seats in parliament and changed its name to the Labour Party, and a Royal Commission on Ecclesiastical Discipline recognized plurality of worship within the Church of England. It is not surprising that a mid-Victorian (as Grahame described himself) should be unsettled, or that his male rural idyll should be very suspicious of women, be seriously worried by motor cars, be terrified of the revolutionary working classes (of the Wild Wood) and, notably in the shape of Badger, assert 'traditional' values. Just how conservative *The Wind in the Willows* is, politically, can be judged by reading Jan Needle's *Wild Wood* (1981), which brilliantly retells the story from the point of view of the downtrodden Wild-Wooders, who revolt against the arrogance of Toad and his upper-class friends.

There are even mysteries about Kenneth Grahame. How did the Secretary of the Bank of England come to write essays for the notorious *Yellow Book*, the avant-garde quarterly which was symbolic of the 'decadent' 1890s? Why did that Secretary suddenly leave the Bank of England under such dramatic circumstances that the Bank's journal expunged all mention of his name from its records? And why, in Holywell Cemetery in Oxford, is his epitaph (by his cousin, Anthony Hope Hawkins, author of *The Prisoner of Zenda*), carved on the *back* of the gravestone that Grahame shares with his son?

But the biggest mystery is why Kenneth Grahame ever wrote the book at all. In 1907 he was a famous, best-selling author of two satirical, witty and ironic books of short stories *about* childhood – emphatically

The other bank: Grahame worked at the Bank of England for twenty-nine years.
This photograph shows the Consols Office in 1894.

not for children – *The Golden Age* (1895) and *Dream Days* (1898). He was at the top of his profession, and his wife was an heiress. He had no need of money, disliked 'notoriety' and thought that writing was 'physical torture ... Why should he undergo it?'[6]

And yet, in the course of perhaps six months, he produced a book of such apparent originality and ingenuity that it became a classic which bridges the gap between children and adults. He was, as we shall see, a remarkable and surprising man.

John S. Sargent 189

2

THE RIVER BANKER:
WHO WAS KENNETH GRAHAME?

Kenneth Grahame's literary agent and friend, Curtis Brown, described him thus:

> One of the handsomest men I ever saw – fairly tall and broad-shouldered, a perfect figure with not a bulge in it, topped by a big, beautiful head, crowned with white hair ... He looked as if he should be the secretary of the greatest bank in the world, with a side interest in letters ...[1]

Which is, of course, exactly what he was.

This distinguished air is caught in John Singer Sargent's portrait of him, and it is no accident that Sargent was the most distinguished portraitist of the period – he painted, among many others, Robert Louis Stevenson, Ellen Terry, Henry James and Theodore Roosevelt. For Kenneth Grahame was well off and privileged from day one – in fact, before day one: he was descended from Robert the Bruce (King of Scots 1306–29), and when he was born, at 32 Castle Street, Edinburgh, on 8 March 1859, the birth was attended by Dr James Young Simpson, the pioneer of the use of chloroform in childbirth.

Kenneth was the third, after Helen and Willie, of four children; his mother died in 1864, shortly after the birth of his brother Roland. His father sent the family to stay with their maternal grandmother, 'Granny Ingles', at a large house, 'The Mount' at Cookham Dean, high above the Thames near Marlow. Although the children were there for little more than a year, Grahame's experiences provided the material for his highly successful, wry, sardonic and witty stories of childhood for adults which were collected in *The Golden Age* and *Dream Days*, the books that made his name. The nearby Quarry Wood, which led down towards the river, emerges in *The Wind in the Willows* as the sinister Wild Wood.

Grahame's father finally abandoned his family, and the finances seem to have been in the hands of his Uncle John. He refused to fund a university career for Kenneth, who instead began work as a clerk in his uncle's firm of parliamentary agents, and then as a 'gentleman clerk' in the Bank of England (he achieved 100% – never equalled – in the entrance examination).[2] The Bank seems to have been an eccentric, not

PREVIOUS PAGE 'A temperate, kindly-looking man [who] had a startled air, [like] a well-bred fawn.' Charcoal drawing of Kenneth Grahame by John Singer Sargent, 1912.

Kenneth Grahame at St Edward's School, Oxford, in August 1870. Grahame is the small bored-looking boy at the feet of the Headmaster (later Warden), the Reverend Algernon Simeon.

to say rowdy place – there are tales of dogfights in the lavatories – and it seems to have given Grahame plenty of time to write (in the Bodleian Library, there is a draft fragment of *The Wind in the Willows* written on Bank paper). After his death, his brother-in-law, Lord Courtauld-Thomson, wrote that 'though possibly these books were not all written during Banking hours, his duties as Secretary may have suggested the titles Golden Age and Dream Days.'[3]

And so this rather reserved, reluctant banker found himself in a London that was the centre of literary and cultural change – and to say that he took advantage of it is an understatement. Conventionally enough, he became a sergeant in the London Scottish Volunteers regiment, and worked in an East End mission for the poor – Toynbee Hall in Stepney. More unconventionally, he became friendly with the remarkable polymath F.J. Furnivall (possibly a model for the Water

The summer face of the Wild Wood – Quarry Wood, Cookham Dean.

Marlow and the Thames from Cookham Dean, where Grahame lived as a child, and where he wrote the final version of *The Wind in the Willows*.

Rat), who ran both a sculling club and the New Shakespeare Society – of which Grahame became the Honorary Secretary.

He also gravitated to more adventurous literary society, writing pieces for another larger-than-life character, W.E. Henley – the model for Robert Louis Stevenson's Long John Silver (and perhaps Mr Toad).

From Henley's *National Observer*, where his fellow contributors included Rudyard Kipling and W.B. Yeats, Grahame moved on to the more outré *Yellow Book*, his essays appearing in eight of its thirteen volumes. A typical piece was 'Long Odds' (July 1895) in which the narrator meets the Secretary of 'some venerable corporation' who has escaped the City of London to live a life of freedom in Venice. 'I could not help thinking, as I parted from him at the Piazzetta steps,' the narrator concludes, 'that … here was one of the sanest creatures I had ever happened upon.'[4] The Water Rat's yearnings were already forming.

He was in distinguished company: his essays also appeared in *Scribner's Magazine* in the USA, illustrated by Maxfield Parrish, and his first collection of essays, *Pagan Papers* (1893), had a frontispiece by Aubrey Beardsley.

But London took up only part of his time. He travelled to Italy (notably to Alassio), and took holidays in Fowey in Cornwall where he sailed with another literary lion – although from another part of the jungle – the novelist, essayist and critic Sir Arthur Quiller-Couch, 'Q'. He also became friends with 'Atky' – Edward Atkinson, the Commodore of the Fowey Yacht Club, and a fellow toy collector: the boating and the boating characters of Cornwall provided rich imagery that was later to surface in *The Wind in the Willows*.

Is this the Water Rat? Scholar, boating man, 'knowledgeable about where to go and what to take along'. F.J. Furnivall in 1902.

The Yellow Book

An Illustrated Quarterly

Volume II   July, 1894

London : Elkin Mathews & John Lane
Boston : Copeland & Day
Agents for the Colonies : Robt. A. Thompson & Co.

ABOVE *The Yellow Book*, July 1894. Grahame's whimsical essays rubbed shoulders in this symbol of *fin-de-siècle* decadence with pieces by the likes of Max Beerbohm, Henry James and Austin Dobson.

OPPOSITE W.E. Henley – editor, mentor, certainly a model for Long John Silver, and possibly for Mr Toad. Grahame described him as 'boisterous and piratic'. Portrait by Spy, *Vanity Fair*, 1896.

THE MAGIC RING

BY KENNETH GRAHAME

Grown-up people really ought to be more careful. Among themselves it may seem but a small thing to give their word and take back their word. For them there are so many compensations. Life lies at their feet, a party-colored india-rubber ball; they may kick it this way or kick it that, it turns up blue, yellow, or green, but always colored and glistening. Thus one sees it happen almost every day, and, with a jest and a laugh, the thing is over, and the disappointed one turns to fresh pleasure, lying ready to his hand. But with those who are below them, whose little globe is swayed by them, who rush to build star-pointing alhambras on their most casual word, they really ought to be more careful.

In this case of the circus, for instance, it was not as if we had led up to the subject. It was they who began it entirely — prompted thereto by the local newspaper. "What, a circus!" said they, in their irritating, casual way; "that would be nice to take the children to. Wednesday would be a good day. Suppose we go on Wednesday. Oh, and pleats are being worn again, with rows of deep braid," etc.

What the others thought I know not; what they said, if they said anything,

ABOVE International success: first published in *Scribner's Magazine* (December 1896) and then in his best-selling *Dream Days*, 'The Magic Ring' celebrates Grahame's lifelong enthusiasm for the circus. (The illustrator, Oliver Herford, has been called the American Oscar Wilde.)

OPPOSITE Grahame's beloved Venice, which he first visited around 1890. 'A fine city, wherein a rat can wander at his ease and take his pleasure.' *The Piazzetta*, *c*.1911 attributed to John Singer Sargent.

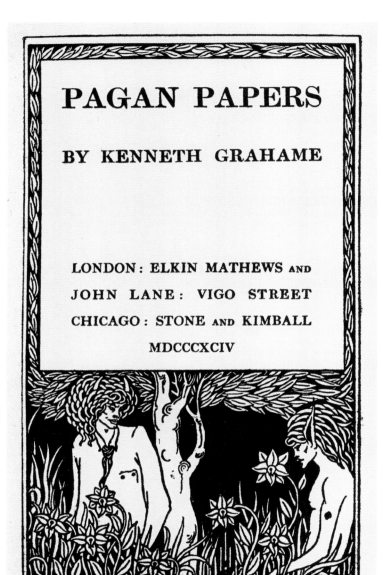

PAGAN PAPERS

BY KENNETH GRAHAME

LONDON: ELKIN MATHEWS AND
JOHN LANE: VIGO STREET
CHICAGO: STONE AND KIMBALL
MDCCCXCIV

Fashionably mystic: the title page of Grahame's breakthrough book, *Pagan Papers*, 1893.

'Q' called Grahame 'eminently a "man's man"' and when he wasn't parading, or sailing, or sculling on the Thames, he might be found striding on the Berkshire Downs. A banking friend, Sidney Ward, described one such expedition, 'one cold, sunny spring'.

> A friend had lent him a fourteenth-century cottage in the main street [of Streatley], and we had a grand twenty-mile walk along the Ridgeway, the subject of his 'Romance of the Road'. If we either of us said clever things that day they are forgotten, but we came home happy and tired, bought some chops and fetched a huge jug of beer from the pub. We cooked our dinner over the open wood fire, and how good the chops were! Then great chunks of cheese, new bread, great swills of beer, pipes, bed, and heavenly sleep![5]

In London, Kenneth lived near the artist Graham Robertson, who described him thus:

> As he strode along the pavements one felt to him as towards a huge St. Bernard or Newfoundland dog, a longing to take him away into the open country where he could be let off the lead. ... He appeared happy enough and made the best of everything, as do the dogs, but he was too big for London and it hardly seemed kind of Fate to keep him there.[6]

And then, in 1897, when he was forty-three, he met the first of the two dynamic women whose influence led to *The Wind in the Willows*. Elspeth Thomson (born 1862 and known as Elsie) came from a distinguished background: she was the daughter of R.W. Thomson, inventor of the pneumatic tyre and the fountain pen, and a sister of Courtauld, Lord Courtauld-Thomson, who left his house, Dorneywood,

'Q' – Sir Arthur Quiller-Couch, novelist, critic, editor of *The Oxford Book of English Verse* and Grahame's yachting companion at Fowey; he wrote Alastair Grahame's obituary for the *Oxford Magazine*. Woodcut by Robert Bryden from *Poets of the Younger Generation* by William Archer, 1902.

to the nation as the residence of 'a senior member of the government' (at the time of writing in 2016 this was the Chancellor of the Exchequer).

Elspeth's widowed mother married John Fletcher Mouton, who was Director of Munitions during the First World War, and Elspeth supported her stepfather's career in politics, although he was somewhat dilatory in allowing her access to her inheritance. After a legal action against him (in which Kenneth was obliquely involved), she and her sister were awarded a settlement of £8,250 (around £1,000,000 today). She also acted as hostess for his literary soirées at his house in Onslow Square in London, meeting luminaries such as Swinburne, Wilde and Browning – and almost certainly Grahame. Sir John Tenniel was a lifelong devotee, and sent her annual Valentines for many years, for example, this from 14 February 1899:

> If you are "Mine" – Oh joy divine!
> I'm certainly "your" Valentine –
> For better or for worser! –
> 'Tis best to shift your little verse
> So simple-sweet, so tersely terse
> And take it VICE-VERSA!!!![7]

And it is signed with the monogram so familiar to the readers of the *Alice* books. One of the surviving portraits of her is, if not by Sargent, by perhaps the next best portrait painter of the day, Frank Dicksee FRA, who was later knighted and became President of the Royal Academy.

She spoke fluent French and Flemish, painted, wrote at least one five-act play (unperformed), much (competent) sentimental verse and published a novella, *Amelia Jane's Ambition*, under the pseudonym of Clarence Onslow. This is a neat, unpatronizing view of working-class life, and has a wry view of her characters very reminiscent of Kenneth's. This sentence, recounting the experience of a baby with a sugar lump could have come from *The Golden Age*: 'For Baby approved of the sugar from the chemical point of view, but disapproved of it from the mechanical,

10, Portsdown Road,
Maida Hill, W.

To my Valentine.

If you are "mine" – Oh, joy divine!
I'm certainly "your" Valentine –
For better or for worser! –
'T is best to shift your little verse –
So simpl'-sweet, so trewly terse.
And take it – VICE-VERSA ! ! ! !

Feb. 14. 1899.

ABOVE Sir John Tenniel's 1899 Valentine poem for Elspeth. Tenniel was a leading political cartoonist, now most famous for being the original illustrator of Lewis Carroll's *Alice* books.

OPPOSITE The woman behind *The Wind in the Willows* – Elspeth Grahame nurtured the writing of the book, and cleverly promoted it after Grahame's death. When they were married, one of Grahame's friends commented: 'you will never be bored again as long as you live.' Portrait by Frank Dicksee, 1881.

and consequently Mother had to go on catching it and re-posting it ...'[8]

To judge from the voluminous correspondence to her that survives, notably after Kenneth's death, she shared his qualities of wit and business acumen, and his capacity to generate affection. (Thomas Hardy confided, in a letter to her (31 August 1907), that he found her poems 'charming'.[9]) She was also, like Kenneth, capable of being whimsical. They had a long correspondence in baby-talk (he was Dino and she was Minkie) which is definitely not for outsiders, and although Kenneth's men-friends disapproved, they were married in Fowey on 22 July 1899, at St Finbarrus's Church. Elspeth shocked Quiller-Couch and the other guests by wearing her old muslin dress to go to watch the dawn – and then wearing the same dress to her wedding. As Grahame's biographer, Peter Green, put it, she 'had a happy indifference to the lesser conventions of the social world'.[10]

The Grahames moved into 16 Durham Villas, Campden Hill, London, and on 18 May 1900 Kenneth wrote to a friend:

> I know you will be relieved & glad to hear that Elsie had a small son yesterday, and that both are doing very well. It was rather unexpected but it all came right, & now it's a blessing to think that she has been saved some weeks more worry. ... She has an excellent nurse ... a real brick. The boy is a big fellow & very good.[11]

Alastair, or 'Mouse', as he was always known, was born partially blind, but grew to be a spirited child (to judge from the substantial volume of letters that his mother preserved). He, naturally, had a governess, and his parents, as was the norm for the time, commonly went on holiday without him (he occasionally complained about their absence).

ABOVE Alastair Grahame as a child, from Patrick Chalmers' *Kenneth Grahame: Life, Letters and Unpublished Work*. The title of this photograph, probably supplied by Elspeth, was: 'The Editor of *The Merrythought*'.

Kenneth's life at the Bank continued, punctuated by two notable incidents. In 1903 one George Robinson came into the Bank and fired three shots at Grahame before being 'overpowered by a quick-witted messenger using a fire hydrant'.[12] Grahame wrote a note to Elspeth (which says a lot about communications at the time):

Bank of England, 24th Nov[r]

Darlin M – Just a line to tell you not to be alarmed at any rumours or statements on posters re. There was a lunatic in here this morning 'shooting free' with a revolver but *nobody* got hurt at all except the lunatic who was secured after some trouble. Yrs ... [13]

Rather more peaceful was the surprise visit to the Bank in 1907 by the Royal Children. As Lord Courtauld-Thomson wrote:

Forty two years ago, four Royal children visited the Bank of England. They were shown the 'Treasure' by my brother-in-law Kenneth Grahame – the then secretary. Each of them signed a £1,000 note, adding the words 'of Wales' to their Christian names. Two of the young Visitors became Kings of England. Prince George, aged five, afterwards Duke of Kent, was not present ... Surprise visit though it was, they had a tea that only Kenneth Grahame could have ordered and only 'the Old Lady of Threadneedle Street' could have provided. [14]

In 1906 the Grahame family moved to 'Mayfield' (now a private school) in Cookham Dean, not far from 'The Mount', while 16 Durham Villas was retained as a pied-à-terre. But not for very long, because in June 1908 Kenneth suddenly left the Bank. Although Grahame had been ill intermittently for a few years, the archivist of the Bank, W. Marston Acres, who had worked with him, wrote:

Exciting times at the Bank: an artist's impression of George Robinson being overpowered at the Bank of England after he had fired three shots at Kenneth Grahame. The front page of the *Daily Graphic*, 26 November, 1903.

MACFARLANE, LANG & CO.'S
OVAL RICH TEA BISCUITS.

THE
DAILY GRAPHIC
ONE PENNY

NO. 4349—Vol. LVI.

LONDON : THURSDAY, NOVEMBER 26, 1903.

REGISTERED AS A NEWSPAPER

THE WEATHER.

"SHOWERS STILL PROBABLE."   (See page 11.)

Sun rises (at Greenwich), 7.46 ; sets, 3.58.
Moon's age at noon, 7 days 7 hours.

THE FISCAL CAMPAIGN.

LORD ROSEBERY IN SOUTH LONDON.

Last night the Earl of Rosebery addressed a Liberal demonstration held in the Surrey Theatre, S.E. He was accompanied by his daughter, the Countess of Crewe. The proceedings had been advertised to begin at half-past seven o'clock, but long before the house was filled from floor to gallery. The chair was taken by Mr. R. K. Causton, M.P. Those present included Sir Henry Fowler, M.P., the Earl and Countess Beauchamp, the Earl of Cork, the Earl and Countess Carrington, Mrs. Asquith, Viscount Hampden, Lady Leconfield, Lord Burghclere, Lord Foot, Lord Wandsworth, Lord Welby, and Sir Barry Johnston.

Lord Rosebery said he was beginning to fear that his best wishes were becoming a bore, and to dwell on the subject after the speeches of the Duke of Devonshire and Lord Goschen might seem superfluous. But the question was one that could not be solved, and because he believed that this new policy aimed a serious if not a fatal blow at our commerce and Empire, he was obliged to confine himself to that subject. The First Lord of the Treasury was more fortunate. He had announced his intention of speaking to-morrow night, and of touching upon the fiscal question. (Laughter.) He, on the other hand, he (Lord Rosebery) was even fortunate than the First Lord, because whatever Mr. Balfour might choose for treatment on Friday night, he could hardly fail to light upon one extremely difficult and full of delicacy in the holding the position which he holds. This issue most concern every patriot and every thinking man until that issue was solved and settled in one way or another, and settled it certainly would be within a comparatively short time.

Issue must be Settled.

The postponement of a dissolution with such an issue in the air was impracticable and impossible, and discussion of other topics was almost, if not quite, impossible. A few months ago we were at peace, so far as we knew—we little knew of the fierce passions agitating the Cabinet. But since then a very prominent statesman had fallen into a gloomy vein with regard to this country. For the last two months he had been unable to see any belfry or bell tower without sounding a knell in it. (Laughter.) At one time he (Lord Rosebery) was rather gloomy himself upon that subject. He was still gloomy—not despondingly gloomy. (Laughter and cheers.) He was gloomy from the point of view of the educational aptitudes of Germany, as compared with England, and then he was taken to task. But seven years was a distant date for some public men, and a quotation from a speech of Mr. Chamberlain at that time directed against their humble servant showed that time worked strange changes, and that their respective positions seemed, to some extent, to have altered. Mr. Chamberlain had proved to his own satisfaction our own ruin over and over again.

A Modern Jeremiah.

We blinded our eyes to facts and figures, and were enjoying universal desolation. (Laughter.) Mr. Chamberlain despaired of everything, and so would the people if they listened to the lamentations of this modern Jeremiah. (Laughter.) We saw the lurid lightning and heard the thunder; at one time

(Continued on page 5.)

THE SHOOTING OUTRAGE AT THE BANK OF ENGLAND: THE OFFICIALS OVERPOWERING THE ASSAILANT WITH THE FIRE HOSE.
(From materials supplied by an eye-witness.) (See page 5.)

821

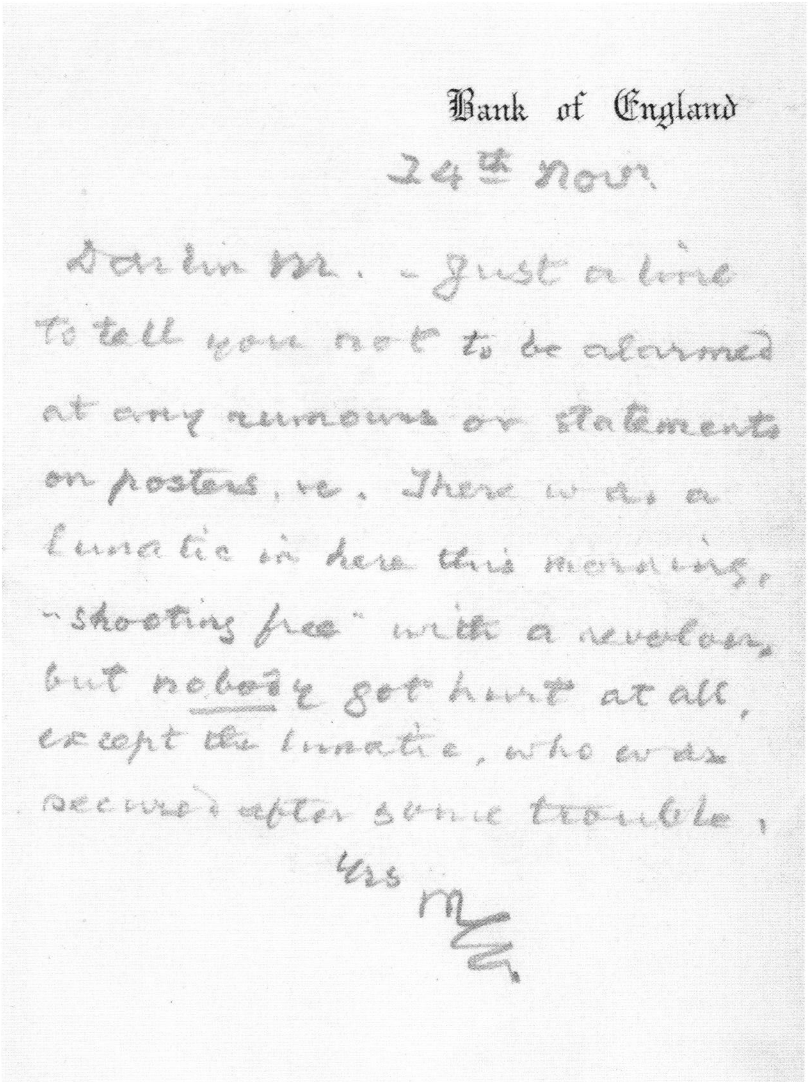

Bank of England

24th Novr.

Darling M. — Just a line
to tell you not to be alarmed
at any rumours or statements
on posters, &c. There was a
lunatic in here this morning,
"shooting free" with a revolver,
but no_body_ got hurt at all,
except the lunatic, who was
secured after some trouble.

Yrs
M

Dino reassures Minkie – although the signature is somewhat ambiguous.
Letter from Kenneth Grahame to Elspeth on Bank of England letterhead, 24 November 1903.

Four banknotes signed by a distinguished group of children: Edward became King Edward VIII; Albert, King George VI; Mary, Princess Royal and Countess of Harewood; and Henry, Duke of Gloucester.

... his retirement had nothing to do with ill-health, but to his resentment of the bullying nature of a Director [Walter Cunliffe] with whom he was discussing some official business, when he was provoked into saying 'You are no gentleman, sir!'[15]

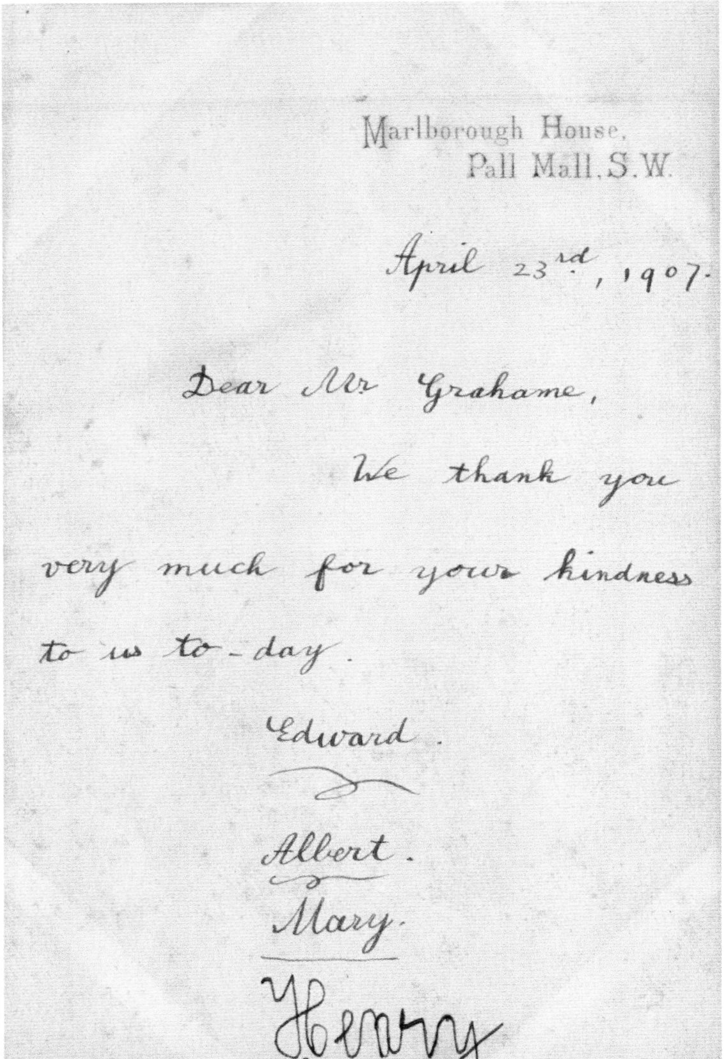

Marlborough House,
Pall Mall. S.W.

April 23rd, 1907.

Dear Mr Grahame,

We thank you very much for your kindness to us to-day.

Edward.

Albert.

Mary.

Henry

A thank-you letter from the Royal Children after their visit to the Bank, which took place two days before Princess Mary's tenth birthday: Edward was twelve, Albert (George) eleven and Henry six.

Given Grahame's success as Secretary, this seems to be an unlikely explanation for the fact that he is not mentioned at all in the official history of the Bank, or that he was awarded only half his expected pension. It remains a mystery.

One historian of the Bank has suggested that *The Wind in the Willows* is based entirely on this affair: the Water Rat is Grahame's brother, Roland, who also worked there (and whose Bank nickname was Ratty), Badger was based on Hammond 'Brock' Chubb, the Secretary who recruited Grahame, Toad on Cunliffe, and so on.[16] Elspeth placed a characteristically positive spin on Kenneth's departure from the Bank. She wrote to her friend Betsey Purves, on 26 July 1908:

> We've disposed of the lease of the London house. ... Mouse is quite charmed with this place (he's been here since Xmas) he has no end of friends in all classes of life – plays chess & is busy all day. He has 2 rabbits & there is a robin that eats out of our hands & lips – The greatest news is that Kenneth has resigned his post – The responsibility was a great strain & was telling on his health ...[17]

But also about this time, during his last days at the Bank, he wrote – or assembled – *The Wind in the Willows* and it seems that all its pieces were already in place.

GREEN BANK HOTEL,

FALMOUTH,

10th may .... 190 7.

My darling Mouse

This is a birth-day letter
to wish you very many happy returns
of the day. I wish we could have
been all together, but we shall
meet again soon, & then we will
have treats. I have sent you two

3

LETTERS TO MOUSE:
DRAFTING THE STORIES

The story of *The Wind in the Willows* really begins in Philadelphia in 1907, with the editor of the popular *Everybody's Magazine*, John O'Hara Cosgrave. *Everybody's* was a fascinating mixture of investigative journalism (or 'muckraking', as President, Theodore Roosevelt called it) – such as exposing the terrible state of tenements owned by Trinity Church in New York City – and substantial fiction by the likes of O. Henry, Booth Tarkington, Kipling and George Bernard Shaw. Cosgrave's rates of pay – $1,000 for 5,000 words – were not to be sneezed at.

The other woman behind *The Wind in the Willows*: the multi-talented Constance Smedley. Portrait from her biography *Crusaders*, 1929.

Cosgrave's 'ideal of literary charm' was Kenneth Grahame, and so he dispatched his agent in England to persuade Grahame to 'break fifteen years of writing silence'. Thus Constance Smedley, the second of the formidable women in Grahame's life, arrived at 'Mayfield': 'I drove over [from Bray] in late summer when the mists of early autumn were invading hedge and lane ...'[1] On the face of it, she seems to have been an unlikely advocate. *The Wind in the Willows* is about male independence, sometimes showing a positive aversion to women. Smedley was a powerful feminist – her *Woman: A Few Shrieks* (1907) is dedicated to 'those women on the fighting line who have had the courage to face ridicule, and the wit to turn the laugh upon their enemies by their indifference to derision.'[2] It has an appendix by Ethel, Mrs Philip Snowden, the prominent left-wing activist, and is as incisive an attack on entrenched male attitudes as any suffragette could hope to launch. Constance was the founder, among much else, of the Lyceum clubs for women writers, and of the Cotswold Players, designed to bring drama to the rural masses. But Constance was also the author of a string of plays and idiosyncratic novels, one of which, *An April Princess* (1903), Grahame had read and admired. It is a very curious performance, consisting of discussions between an egocentric young woman and her various friends and suitors (her 'Prince' lives in Cookham), but perhaps it appealed to Kenneth's (or Elspeth's) whimsical side. Constance became a friend of the family, and at that first meeting it seems likely that she recognized that Grahame, despite his protestations, already had a book in embryo.

Precisely how that book originated is not entirely clear, largely because the fullest accounts we have come from Patrick Chalmers' *Kenneth Grahame: Life, Letters and Unpublished Work* (1933) and Elspeth's best-selling *First Whisper of* The Wind in the Willows (1944). Both books

THIS BOOK

is offered

To those women on the
fighting line who have
had the courage to face
ridicule, and the wit to
turn the laugh upon their
enemies by their
indifference to
derision

WOMAN:

A Few
Shrieks!

*Setting forth the necessity of Shrieking
till the Shrieks be heard.*

BY **X**

With an Appendix by
Mrs. PHILIP SNOWDEN

Incisive arguments rather than shrieks, but still on the face of it, a book that seems unlikely to have recommended Smedley to Grahame. Title page of *Woman: A Few Shrieks!*, by Constance Smedley, 1907.

were produced under the iron supervision of Elspeth, who was intent on preserving, as we would now say, the 'brand', and romanticizing her son, and so it is difficult to extract fact from fiction. (The extent of her editing, or altering, contributions to *First Whisper* worried her publishers. As J.A. White of Methuen wrote to her: 'I am not *quite* comfortable about the deletion or alterations here and there of words and phrases in the letters.')[3]

It seems clear enough, however, that the book really did begin with bedtime stories told by Kenneth to 'Mouse'. In 1903, Kenneth described them to Elspeth (in their baby-talk dialect):

> – there was a story in which a mole, a beever a badjer & a water rat was characters & I got them terribly mixed up as I went along but ee always straitened them out & remembered wich was wich ... I erd im telling [the nanny] artewards 'and do you no ... the mole saved up all his money and went and bought a motor car!' ... You will perceive by this that Mr. Mole has been goin' the pace since he first went his simple boatin spedition wif the water rat.[4]

In May 1904, the Grahames were late for a dinner party because Kenneth was, according to the maid, 'up in the night-nursery telling Master Mouse some ditty or another about a Toad'.[5] This anecdote was elaborated by Elspeth into a scene at a Scottish castle where they were holidaying, and a guest overhears the story being told:

> I heard two of the most beautiful voices, one relating a wonderful story, and the other, soft as the south wind blowing, sometimes asking for an explanation ... at others laughing like a whole chime of bells – the loveliest duet possible ...[6]

Constance Smedley's account at least confirms the storytelling: 'Every evening Mr Grahame told Mouse an unending story, dealing with the adventures of the little animals whom they met on their river journeys.'[7]

Grahame, then, had the basic plan of the book – beginning with Mole's trip on the river, but he had more than that: if Constance visited him at the end of August, he had already written 12,000 words – eleven of the fifteen letters that he had written to Mouse, telling the story of Toad's adventures.

The letters are clearly a continuation of the bedtime stories; the first was written from the Green Bank Hotel, Falmouth, on 10 May 1907. After some preliminaries, wishing 'My Darling Mouse' a happy birthday ('I wish we could have been together, but we shall meet again soon & then we shall have treats') and listing the books and toys they have sent him, the letter goes on: 'Have you heard about the Toad? ... [H]e got out of the window early one morning and went off to a town called Buggleton & went to the Red Lion Hotel & there he found a party that had just motored down from London ...'[8] The Bodleian Library files contain an undated letter from Mouse, referring to one of the letters, presumably one written in September, 1907, when the 13th of the month was a Friday: 'Dear Daddy, we have received the Toad letter / on a Friday and it was such a fine day that everybody forgot that it was unlucky. From your affectionate Mouse.'[9]

Altogether the letters run to about 18,000 words, and over the next few months Grahame expanded them into the 25,000 published words describing Toad's adventures – Chapters VIII, X, XI and XII: the last of these – for Grahame was really in his stride by this time – needed only 500 additional words.

ABOVE View of Falmouth, c.1900. Grahame had a great liking for small Cornish seaside towns.

OVERLEAF The first of the letters to Mouse: Toad's adventures have already started! Letter from Kenneth Grahame to Alastair, Falmouth, 10 May 1907.

There are some oddities about the letters. The first that might strike the twenty-first-century parent is that Kenneth and Mouse were not on holiday together – while his parents were at Falmouth or Fowey, Mouse was in Littlehampton with his nurse. Ten of the letters are from Durham Villas to Cookham Dean, and of these, two were written on Fridays and one on Saturday – which suggests that Grahame did not always go home, even at the weekends.

GREEN BANK HOTEL,

FALMOUTH,

.... 10th may .... 190 7.

My darling Mouse

This is a birth-day letter
to wish you very many happy return
of the day. I wish we could have
been all together, but we shall
meet again soon, & then we will
have <u>treats</u>. I have sent you two
picture-books, one about Brer
Rabbit, from Daddy, & one about
some other animals, from mummy
and we have sent you a boat,

painted red, with mast & sails, to
sail in the round pond by the
windmill _ & mummy has sent you
a boat-hook to catch it when it
comes to shore. Also mummy has
sent you some sand-toys to play
in the sand with, and a card-game.

Have you heard about the
Toad? He was never taken prisoner
by brigands at all. It was all a
horrid low trick of his. He wrote
that letter himself _ the letter saying
that a hundred pounds must be
put in the hollow tree. And he got
out of the window early one morning,
— went off to a town called Buggleton
— went to the Red Lion Hotel & there
he found a party that had just
motored down from London, &
while they were having breakfast he

Mouse's reply!

ABOVE Then and now: Grahame wrote from this hotel to propose to Elspeth – and they spent some of their honeymoon here.

OVERLEAF Even if they were not on holiday at the same place, father and son could share Toad's adventures. Here is the end of the barge-man story.

Even more oddly, after the sixth letter, the salutation changes from 'My Dearest Mouse' to 'My dear Robinson' or 'Dear Robinson'. As Michael Gooderson explains:

> This followed Mouse's announcement that he was changing his name to Michael Robinson ... There are no words of affection [in the letters that follow], since Grahame maintained that he was incapable of familiarity towards a complete stranger.[10]

a shirt, you very silly old woman!" Then the
toad lost his temper, & quite forgot himself
& said "Don't you dare to speak to your
betters like that! And don't call me a silly
old woman! I'm no more an old woman
than you are yourself, you common, low,
vulgar bargee!" Then the bargee looked
closely at him, & cried out "Why, no, I can
see you're not really a washerwoman at
all! You're nothing but an old toad!"
Then he grabbed the toad by one hind.leg
& one fore.leg, & swung him round & sent
him flying through the air

Like that - Splosh!!
He found himself head.over.ears in the water

When the toad came to the surface he
wiped the water out of his eyes & struck out
for the shore; but the woman's dress he was
wearing got round his legs, & made it very
hard work. When at last he was safely on
the tow.path again, he saw the barge
disappearing in the distance, & the man
looking back & laughing at him. This
made Mr. Toad mad with rage. He tucked
the wet skirt up well under his arms,
& ran as hard as he could along the path

passed the barge, & ran on till he
overtook the horse that was towing it, and
unfastened the tow-rope, & jumped on
the horse's back, & dug his heels into its
sides, & off they went at a gallop!
He took one look back as they went, & he
saw that the barge had run — into the
opposite bank of the canal, & stuck, & the
bargee was shaking his fist at him &
calling out · Stop, stop, stop!! But the
toad never stopped, but only laughed
& galloped on & on & on, across country,
over fields & hedges, until he had left the
canal, & the barge, & the bargee, miles &
miles behind him.

I am afraid the Gipsy will have to
wait till the next letter.

Your affectionate
Daddy

I am so glad to hear you have
been out in a motor boat

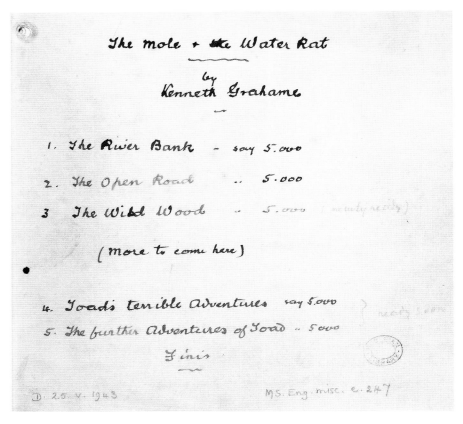

The title page of the Bodleian manuscript – with a first attempt at a title.

Given that Mouse later referred to Grahame in letters home as 'Inferiority', and the fact that Robinson was the name of the man who had shot at him at the Bank makes this small quirk take on a somewhat sinister aspect.

So, with the letters as a foundation, Grahame, the reluctant writer, looked around for ways to build a book.

Grahame – rather Badger-like at sixty. Photograph by Lady Ottoline Morrell, *c*.1920.

MESSING ABOUT IN BOOKS:
BUILDING *THE WIND IN THE WILLOWS*

Grahame, despite his shy and conventional persona, had a remarkably well-informed mind, and an impish sense of humour. He wove into his book portraits of places that he loved (the water mill where Rat and Toad picnic could be at Golant on the River Fowey; the god Pan appears at Hurley backwater, near Marlow) and poked gentle fun at his friends.

For example, it has been variously suggested that Toad is based on people as diverse as King Edward VII, Horatio Bottomley, Alastair Grahame or even the radically inclined Bishop Charles Gore. But a

ABOVE The real Mr Toad? Sir Charles Day-Rose Bt (1847–1913) –
Scottish-Canadian banker, railway promoter, racehorse owner,
member of the Jockey Club and the National Hunt Committee,
MP for Newmarket, yachtsman, President of the Royal Aero Club,
Chairman of the RAC, driver of fast cars and friend of Grahame.
Sketch by 'Spy' in *Vanity Fair*, 30 June 1904.

PREVIOUS PAGE Where Pan pipes? Grahame wrote: 'In the hushed
recesses of Hurley backwater where the canoe may be paddled
almost under the tumbling comb of the weir, he is to be looked
for; there the god pipes with the freest abandonment.' This was
one of Jerome K. Jerome's favourite places, too. Illustration by A.R.
Quinton from Hilaire Belloc, *The Historic Thames*, 1907.

Toad's favourite car? Day-Rose's Mercedes Simplex Tourer, *c.*1904 – at least 5.3 litres!

prime candidate (nominated by *Burke's Peerage*) might be Sir Charles Day-Rose, 'an entertaining, passionate man, who was always having crazes for unusual activities. ... He was extremely proud of his large open car, a 1904 Mercedes Simplex Tourer. It had a six-cylinder engine and a very long bonnet,' and Day-Rose owned a Thames-side house of 'mellow red brick', Hardwick House, near Whitchurch-on-Thames.[1]

Toad Hall? Hardwick House, near Whitchurch-on-Thames contains a bedchamber used by Elizabeth I – and one of only twenty-seven Real Tennis courts in England, installed by Day-Rose in 1907. From Hilaire Belloc, *The Historic Thames*, 1907.

Kenneth was a frequent visitor – and is said to have spent time lying on the river bank watching the water rats. (Henry James also visited, joining in Sir Charles' literary soirées, and featured the same house in the opening chapter of *Portrait of a Lady*, published in 1881.)

It is perhaps not surprising that *The Wind in the Willows* has the reputation of being a river book, given that it opens with a panegyric on boats. As the Water Rat says: 'Believe me, my young friend, there is *nothing* – absolutely nothing – half so much worth doing as simply messing about in boats.'

"'Nice?' It's the only thing," said the Water Rat solemnly, as he leant forward for his stroke. "Believe me, my young friend, there is nothing — absolutely nothing — half so much worth doing, as simply messing about in boats. Simply messing," he went on dreamily: "messing — about — in — boats; messing ——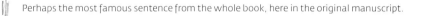

"Look ahead, Rat!" cried the Mole, suddenly.

It was too late. The boat struck the bank full tilt. The dreamer, the joyous oarsman, lay on his back at the bottom of the boat, his heels in the air.

"—— about in boats — or with boats," the Rat went on composedly, picking himself up with a pleasant laugh. "In or out of 'em, it doesn't matter. Nothing seems really to matter, that's the charm of it. Whether you get off, or whether you don't; whether you arrive at your destination, or whether you reach somewhere else, or whether you never get anywhere at all, you're always busy, & you never

Perhaps the most famous sentence from the whole book, here in the original manuscript.

But Grahame was not simply indulging himself: boating on the Thames towards the end of the century ('The bank is so crowded nowadays,' observes the Rat[2]) was immensely popular, and there was a popular literature to go along with it.

The most famous book in this genre is Jerome K. Jerome's *Three Men in a Boat* (1889). The Jeromes and the Grahames – perhaps needless to say –

Toad is repressed! Badger orders the latest motor car to be returned to the garage. This is also the key scene in Jan Needle's *Wild Wood* – when the driver of the car, Baxter the Ferret, is thrown out of work. E.H. Shepard's view of Toad Hall.

One of the several incidents in Jerome K. Jerome's *Three Men in a Boat* that has an echo in *The Wind in the Willows* – J, the absent-minded poet, rows into a boat full of ancient fishermen. Illustration by A. Frederics from the 1889 edition.

knew each other, and Grahame lived quite close to Jerome, off Chelsea Bridge Road in London, when *Three Men in a Boat* was being written. The three main characters of *Three Men* may seem curiously familiar to readers of *The Wind in the Willows*. J, the narrator, is a poet who can be absent-minded when steering a boat; George is a clerk 'who goes to sleep at a bank from ten to four each day' and Harris is 'a well-made man of about number one size', given to misadventures and to singing comic songs.[3] The books even share locations – notably Quarry Wood, although Jerome's portrait of it is much more cheerful than Grahame's.

But the river book is soon superseded in the second chapter of *The Wind in the Willows*, 'The Open Road', by the caravanning book. Caravanning was another contemporary craze: the Caravan Club was founded in 1907. Its inspiration was Gordon Stables, a prolific novelist for children, who built one of the first 'recreational' caravans – a 'land-yacht' called 'The Wanderer' (it was something of a monster – 20 feet

An Ugly Ascent: Gordon Stables, the caravan, and the romance of the mountains. What Toad was saved from by the appearance of the motor car! Illustration from G. Stables, *The Cruise of the Land Yacht 'Wanderer'*, 1886.

long and pulled by two horses). In *Leaves from the Log of a Gentleman Gypsy in Wayside Camp and Caravan* (1891), Stables takes the reader inside:

> This after cabin is also the pantry and kitchen. Here are the racks for plates, dishes, cups, saucers, glasses etc. Above are enclosed shelves; by this is the filter. Even the dog gets filtered water. These rows of neat, white, scarlet-braided pockets contain the towels, clean dusters, etc. ... And everything is in its place; we can find anything, even in the dark. The greatest regularity must prevail in a caravan, and cleanliness and beauty must everywhere reign supreme.

Stables was first inspired by seeing a 'bright yellow caravan, the wheels picked out in vermilion …'[4] – and here is Toad, who has much of Stables' enthusiasm, and the same taste in colours:

> He led the way to the stable-yard …, the Rat following with a most mistrustful expression; and there, drawn out of the coach house into the open, they saw a gipsy caravan, shining with newness, painted a canary-yellow picked out with green, and red wheels …
>
> It was indeed very compact and comfortable. Little sleeping bunks – a little table that folded up against the wall – a cooking-stove, lockers, bookshelves, a bird-cage with a bird in it; and pots, pans, jugs and kettles of every size and variety.

Stables also had a coachman and a valet in attendance, and it is difficult not to see Grahame poking gentle fun when Toad goes to bed with the remark: 'This is the real life for a gentleman!' and then stays in bed in the morning and lets the others do the work.[5]

And then …

> … the magnificent motor-car, immense, breath-snatching, passionate, with its pilot tense and hugging his wheel, possessed all earth and air for a fraction of a second …

and possesses Toad, too. (After the wreck of the caravan, the Rat shouts after the departing car: 'You scoundrels, you highwaymen, you – you – road-hogs!' In the holograph, it is 'you stockbrokers!'.[6])

The resemblance of Toad in his motoring-goggles on the spine of the first edition of *The Wind in the Willows* (see page 90) to the character on the cover of G. Sidney Paternoster's *The Motor Pirate* (1903) is no accident.

Arthur Rackham's illustrations for *The Wind in the Willows* (1940) were the last work of his brilliant career, which included backgrounds for Walt Disney's *Snow White and the Seven Dwarfs*.

econd, flung an enveloping cloud of dust that blinded &
nwrapped them utterly, & they dwindled to a speck in the far
distance, becoming a droning bee once more.

The old grey horse, dreaming, as he plodded along, of his quiet paddock,
in a new raw situation such as this simply abandoned himself
to his natural emotions. Rearing, plunging, backing steadily, in spite
of all the Mole's efforts at his head, & all the Mole's lively language
directed at his better feelings, he drove the cart backwards
towards the deep ditch at the side of the road. It wavered an
instant — then there was a heart-rending crash — & the canary-
coloured cart, their pride & their joy, lay on its side in the
ditch, an irredeemable wreck.

The Rat danced up & down in the road, simply transported
with passion. "You villains!" he shouted, shaking both fists.
"You scoundrels, you highwaymen, you - you - stockbrokers! —
I'll have the law of you! I'll report you! I'll take you through
all the Courts!" His home-sickness had quite slipped away
from him, & for the moment he was the skipper of the canary.

45

| A page from the manuscript of *The Wind in the Willows* showing the Water Rat's original insult – 'stockbrokers!' rather than 'road-hogs!' – a term that dates from the 1890s.

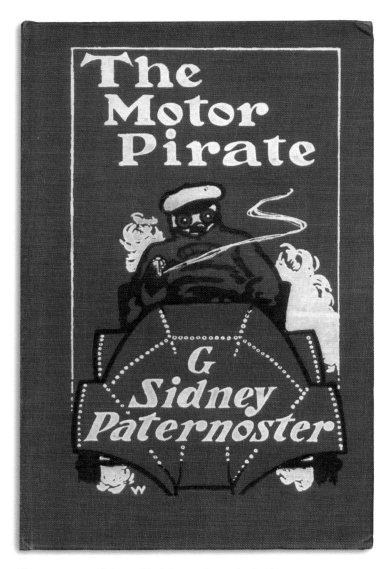

The new romance of the road! And the story is exactly what it says – the masked motorist hijacking cars. *The Motor-Pirate* by G. Sydney Paternoster (1903).

Car thrillers and romances were very much in vogue; notable examples are C.N. and A.M. Williamson's *The Princess Passes – A Romance of a Motor* (1904) and *The Lightning Conductor: The Strange Adventures of a Car* (1904) – where romance is combined with a tour of France and Italy (including Alassio). Equally, it seems very unlikely that Grahame did not read Florence and Bertha Upton's contribution to the genre, *The Gollywogg's Auto-Go-Cart* (1901), to Mouse. In the innocent days before the character became corrupted into a racial stereotype – Florence Upton was horrified to watch the process – the Gollywogg was the amiable hero, a very Toad-like figure, who, in this book, races around the country in his car, is put in prison, escapes using a rope made of his friend's cape and ends up in a river.

The three chapters, 'The Wild Wood', 'Mr Badger' and 'Dulce Domum' are suffused with a deep nostalgia for an England that was passing – characteristic of Richard Jefferies, A.E. Houseman, Rudyard Kipling and, of course, Thomas Hardy. The scene at Mole's house when the field-mice sing a perhaps surprisingly Christian carol, 'Villagers all this Frosty Tide' (since set to music in several versions), is reminiscent of *Under the Greenwood Tree* (1872). But perhaps the book that influenced Grahame most, or at least which chimes most closely with his preoccupations, was E.V. Lucas's anthology, *The Open Road: A Little Book for Wayfarers*, first published in 1899, and in its twelfth edition by 1907. Its 'Argument' reads:

> This little book aims at nothing but providing companionship on the road for city-dwellers who make holiday. It has no claims to completeness of any kind: it is just a garland of good or enkindling poetry and prose fitted to urge folk into the open air … to slip easily from the pocket beneath a tree or among the heather.[7]

Carol singers from the lost traditional rural world: Grahame, ably abetted by Shepard, in Thomas Hardy mode. (Elspeth corresponded with Emma Hardy soon after she was married.)

In it we find Shelley's 'The Invitation' – 'Away, away, from men and towns, / To the wild wood and the downs –'; and his 'Hymn of Pan' – 'Listening to my sweet pipings / The wind in the reeds and the rushes …'; Keats's 'Happy is England' – 'Yet do I sometimes feel a languishment / For skies Italian'; and W.E. Henley's 'The Pretty Washerwoman', which, of course, Grahame rather savagely satirizes in the Barge-woman: 'Her round arms white with lather, / Her elbows fresh and red, / Her mouth the rosiest of buds, / Who would not risk a shower of suds / To kiss her dainty head?'. There are extracts from Richard Jefferies' *The Story of My Heart* ('The Hill Pantheist') at which Grahame had poked rather ambivalent fun in 'Loafing' in *Pagan Papers* (after several paragraphs of purple-passage nature-mysticism, he decides that beer 'is a thing of deity – beer is divine').[8]

If there is a mystic element to these rural idylls, the mysticism of 'The Piper at the Gates of Dawn' taps into the lush neo-pagan *fin-de-siècle* romanticism of the Rossettis, Wilde and Beardsley. This was one of the most popular chapters at the beginning of the century (the Australian Prime Minister Alfred Deakin particularly approved of it). Grahame's Pan is a great deal less savage and ambivalent than contemporary representations, but comes close to homoeroticism with the description of the god's rippling muscles and the 'splendid curves of the shaggy limbs'.[9]

Probably the last chapter to be written, 'Wayfarers All' may be the most personal to Grahame, as the Rat struggles between his loyalty to home and convention, and the temptations of adventure. Whereas in his 1895 essay, 'Long Odds', the escape to a gorgeously evoked Italy was seen as quintessentially sane, now it is a sign of madness: Mole, 'looking into [Rat's] eyes saw that they were glazed and set and streaked and shifting grey – not his friend's eyes, but the eyes of some other animal!'[10] The fact that it is the once-adventurous Mole who subdues the would-be rebel – just as Toad is finally subdued – lends the book an ultimately negative and defeatist tone. Perhaps Grahame, that very private man, was writing out his deepest frustrations.

OVERLEAF William Hyde's endpapers for E.V. Lucas's anthology, *The Open Road*, 1899 – which sums up the dreams of frustrated city-dwellers (and bankers).

5

DOWN STREAM:
WHAT HAPPENED AFTERWARDS

And so the book was finished – but how it came to be published is another mystery. Constance Smedley (now Mrs Maxwell Armfield) says in her autobiography, *Crusaders*, that 'it was sent' to *Everybody's*:

> Mr. Cosgrave was delighted with it, but the owners of the magazine had other ideas. They felt that a fairy story, however beautifully woven was out of character with the style of the magazine ... Most reluctantly Mr. Cosgrave explained the awkward situation and returned the manuscript.[1]

What is slightly odd about this, is that when Constance wrote to Grahame on 30 June 1909, hoping to arrange a meeting with Cosgrave, who was in London, her letter implies that Grahame had not heard about Cosgrave's problem with it:

> A very great Penitent is so desirous of meeting you if you will heap coals of fire on a mistaken head ... Mrs Cosgrave has christened her cottage on a Canadian lake, "Toad Hall": & her husband is a sad man. He just couldn't see it in Everybody's – didn't dare – after the way of editors – publish anything quite so utterly different ...[2]

Be that as it may, sometime either before or after Cosgrave's rejection of the book, Constance ('with that kindly enthusiasm of hers') had introduced Grahame to Curtis Brown – initiating a lifelong friendship between the two families. Brown tried the book (tentatively titled *The Wind in the Reeds*), as he put it,

> with magazine editors all over England and America. They thought it too fantastic and wouldn't have it. Then it went to Charles Scribner ... He said it wouldn't go, but just then he got a letter from Theodore Roosevelt, who was very fond of Kenneth Grahame, and had read the MS., saying that he heard the book had been submitted, and that it was such a beautiful thing that Scribner *must* publish it.[3]

It is a good story, and Roosevelt and his family were certainly fans of *The Golden Age* and *Dream Days*, but the mystery is, how did Roosevelt come to read it? Brown clearly didn't send it to him or he would have mentioned it; could it have been Constance, or Elspeth? The simple fact seems to be that he had *not* read it. On 10 October 1908 Grahame

The Uplands Minchinhampton
June 30th 1909

Dear Mr Grahame
A very great Penitent is
so desirous of meeting you if
you will heap coals of fire on
a mistaken Head. I hear with joy
The Wind in the Willows is a huge
success in America — Mrs Cosgrave
has christened her cottage on a
Canadian lake "Toad Hall": & her
husband is a sad man.
He just couldn't see it in
Everybody's — didn't dare —
after the way of Editors — publish
anything quite so utterly
different — — But he longs

Constance Smedley writes to Grahame on 30 June, 1909 from Minchinhampton in the Cotswolds, making the mystery of the publication of *The Wind in the Willows* even more mysterious.

sent Roosevelt a copy 'of the English edition' (published that month by Methuen) – but it had not arrived in Washington by 22 October, when Roosevelt wrote: 'as I have never read anything of yours yet that I haven't enjoyed to the full, I am safe in thanking you heartily in advance.' He was indeed safe, for two months later, on 7 January 1909, he wrote to Grahame at 16 Durham Villas:

> My mind moves in ruts, as I suppose most minds do, and at first I could not reconcile myself to the change from the ever delightful Harold and his associates, and so for some time I could not accept the toad, the mole, the water-rat and the badger as substitutes. But after a while, Mrs Roosevelt and two of the boys, Kermit and Ted, all quite independently, got hold of 'The Wind among the Willows' and took such delight in it that I began to feel I might have to revise my judgement. Then Mrs. Roosevelt read it aloud to the younger children and I listened now and then. Now I have read it and re-read it ... I am almost more fond of it than your previous books.[4]

Hardly the words of a man who was instrumental in getting the book published in the first place!

Meanwhile, Curtis Brown had taken the manuscript to the London publisher Algernon Methuen, who, as Brown wrote, 'didn't believe in the book enough to pay a guaranteed advance on it; but on the other hand he agreed to excellent rising royalties, just in case the book *should* fulfil my dreams'.[5] But then there was the question of the title. The typescript in the Bodleian Library is entitled *The Mole and the Water-Rat*; the book was advertised as *The Wind in the Reeds*, but this was rather too close to W.B. Yeats's collection *The Wind Among the Reeds* (1899); the present title may well have been coined by Methuen. In the event, the

American edition of *The Wind in the Willows* was published four days *before* the English one – and the copy that Grahame inscribed for Alastair is one of these.

There is an intriguing postscript, which makes Constance Smedley's account all the more mystifying. The year after *The Wind in the Willows* appeared, Curtis Brown met Cosgrave (whom he described as 'a most loveable and impulsive red-head').

> After 'The Wind in the Willows' had been out in book form for a year, he came over to London, and dined at my house, and over the cigars divulged the fact that he had a grievance. 'What devil possessed you,' he said, 'to keep you from offering me the serial rights of the book I admire more than any lately published … I mean "The Wind in the Willows."'
>
> I told him that, to the best of my belief, it had been offered to him. He said he would bet a barrel of apples to a penny that I was wrong. The next day my secretary produced from the file an impassioned personal letter from me to Cosgrave telling him that he really *must* take that serial. I handed the letter to him, and he said, after a moment of what I took to be silent prayer: 'What kind of apples do you like best?'[6]

So, who *did* send the manuscript to Cosgrave – and could he have rejected it *twice* and then forgotten about it?

If *The Wind in the Willows* sold slowly to begin with, its fame soon spread worldwide. On 23 April 1909, Grahame wrote in reply to the Australian Prime Minister, Alfred Deakin: 'If I have ever received a pleasanter or more encouraging appreciation, I do not remember it.'[7] And it was not long before the book was established as a family favourite and Grahame became, once again, a reluctant celebrity.

THE WHITE HOUSE
WASHINGTON

Personal.   January 17, 1909.

My dear Mr. Grahame:

My mind moves in ruts, as I suppose most minds do,
and at first I could not reconcile myself to the change
from the ever delightful Harold and his associates, and
so for some time I could not accept the toad, the mole,
the water-rat and the badger as substitutes. But after
a while Mrs. Roosevelt and two of the boys, Kermit and
Ted, all quite independently, got hold of "The Wind Among
the Willows" and took such delight in it that I began to
feel that I might have to revise my judgment. Then Mrs.
Roosevelt read it aloud to the younger children, and I
listened now and then. Now I have read it and reread
it, and have come to accept the characters as old friends;
and I am almost more fond of it than of your previous
books. Indeed, I feel about going to Africa very much
as the seafaring rat did when he almost made the water-

Moving in the highest circles. One of US President Theodore Roosevelt's letters to Grahame, 17 January 1909.

wish to
rat forsake everything and start wandering!

I felt I must give myself the pleasure of telling
you how much we had all enjoyed your book.

With all good wishes,

Sincerely yours,

Theodore Roosevelt

Mr. Kenneth Grahame,
    16 Durham Villas,
        Kensington W.,
            London, England.

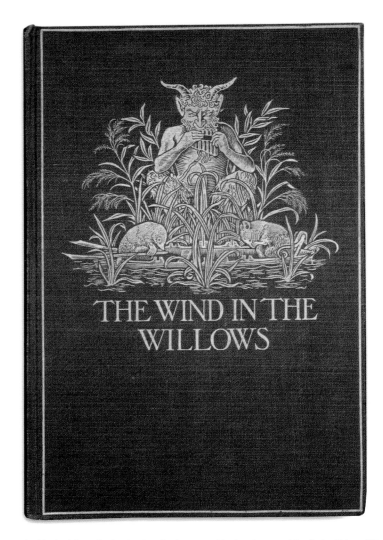

Ambivalent from the beginning: the image on the front cover of the first edition of *The Wind in the Willows* (Methuen, 1908) stresses the mystic and the rural; the picture of Toad in motoring goggles on the spine promises farce.

In 1910 the Grahames moved to 'Boham's', a farmhouse on the Berkshire Downs in the village of Blewbury, which, although far from the Thames, has many ponds and springs – and access to open walking country. Kenneth published virtually nothing, although he was working on *The Cambridge Book of Poetry for Children*: the first of two volumes was published in 1916. This collection cheerfully turns its back on nineteenth-century traditions: there is no shortage in children's poetry, Grahame wrote in the 'Preface', of 'dead fathers and mothers, dead brothers and sisters, dead uncles and aunts, dead puppies and kittens, dead birds, dead flowers, dead dolls ... I have turned off this mournful tap of tears as far as possible ...'[8]

But elsewhere in his life there was tragedy. His old friend Edward Atkinson drowned in 1911, and then Alastair, after a succession of unhappy experiences at schools through his teenage years, was found dead on the railway line at Port Meadow in Oxford in 1918. The inquest recorded a verdict of 'accidental death', although many (including 'Q') have suspected that it was suicide. The Grahames left the country and toured Italy for three years, Kenneth becoming an expert on architecture and 'the table and the bin'. They witnessed Mussolini's March on Rome in 1922: Elspeth wrote to her brother, in characteristically lucid terms: 'we used to hear the Fascists cracking the skulls of the Socialists at street corners, with cannons at both ends of the bridges and snipers shooting over the high wall surrounding the courtyard of the G.P.O.'[9] (The files in the Bodleian contain a rather plaintive 1922 letter from Whittaker's, Kenneth's tailors, worried that they have not supplied him of late![10])

Kenneth and Elspeth returned to England in 1923 and settled at Church Cottage, Pangbourne, both of them semi-reclusive and given to

And
a River went out from
Eden

(*From a drawing by W. Graham Robertson*)

consuming large quantities of claret and champagne. Elspeth got into the habit of answering Kenneth's considerable fan mail. For example, in the first chapter of *The Wind in the Willows*, the Otter alludes in passing to a 'good story about Toad and the lock-keeper'[11] and in 1923, one Thomas Goodman of Wing, Leighton Buzzard, wished to know more about it. Elspeth (probably) replied: 'I'm afraid I must not tell you the story. ... The fact is, they both lost their tempers, and said things they much regretted afterwards. They are now friends again, so we have all agreed to let the matter drop,' and Kenneth signed the letter.[12]

Curtis Brown had sent *The Wind in the Willows* 'to manager after manager in the hope of getting it put on the stage. "Too whimsical," they said, "and quite impossible to represent [the characters] in believable costumes."'[13] Then in 1921 he turned to A.A. Milne, whose *Toad of Toad Hall* was eventually produced – at the Liverpool Playhouse – in 1929. Milne's characteristically witty 'Introduction' points out that what works in a book doesn't necessary work on the stage, and so he removes the reflective chapters – but not without a rather obsequious nod towards the superiority of these 'adult' elements.

> Of course I have left out all the best parts of the book; and for that, if he has any knowledge of the theatre, Mr. Grahame will thank me. With a Rat and Mole from the Green Room Club [a club for actors founded by Sir Henry Irving in 1877], a Baby Otter from Conti [the Italia Conti theatre school was founded in 1911], a Pan from Clarkson's [costumier], and a

The frontispiece to the first edition of *The Wind in the Willows* (Methuen, 1908) by Grahame's friend Graham Robertson. Robertson had discussed various titles with him, but gave up: 'It may come – as you say – while shaving – yet ever I shave and it comes not.'

wind (off) whispering in the reeds of Harker [scene painter and designer; his friend Bram Stoker named the hero of *Dracula* after him], we are not going to add any fresh thrill to the thrill which the loveliness of *The Piper at the Gates of Dawn* has already given its readers.[14]

It also took some time to find the ideal illustrator. The first, the American Paul Bransom (1913), interpreted the animal-named characters literally as animals, with a rather grotesque effect. The second, another American, Nancy Bernhart (1922), and the third, Wyndham Payne (1927), gave them human size and human clothing – and Grahame was amused by the latter. But the illustrations most commonly associated with the book are by E.H. Shepard, who visited Grahame and took advice from him in 1930. Methuen published the Shepard edition in November 1931, and there was a special edition of around 200 copies, signed by Shepard and Grahame. The original illustrations were sold at the Sporting Gallery (27 November– 19 December) and Shepard wrote to Grahame offering him first choice of any of the drawings as a gift.[15] Shepard made a mistake in illustrating Chapter II, which throws some light on publishing practices (see page 96). The text reads: 'Mole ... got into the boat and took the sculls, while the Rat settled himself comfortably in the stern.' The first Shepard edition (1931) has Rat at the sculls:

this was corrected in the 2nd and 3rd thus editions (40th edition, 1932 and 43rd edition, 1933) so that Mole is at the sculls. However, subsequent editions reverted to the incorrect illustration right up to the 101st edition

The Swan Inn, Pangbourne, a little upriver from Church Cottage, Grahame's home from 1924. Illustration from Hilaire Belloc's *The Historic Thames*, 1907.

Even the best illustrators make mistakes – in this case, twice! Having re-drawn the picture in 1932, so that Mole is sculling (as described in the story), when Shepard came to colour the line-drawings in 1969, he used the original picture which incorrectly shows Rat at the oars!

in 1951. At some stage after this date, the revised illustration was once again used ... and some subsequent reprints are correct. The lack of any pattern suggests that the two plates were at the disposal of the printers who were unaware that they were not identical.[16]

Kenneth died peacefully in 1932. After his funeral at Pangbourne where there were 'flowers sent by children from all over the country...',[17] his body was taken to Holywell Cemetery in Oxford, and interred with Alastair's. Antony Hope's eulogy to Kenneth was added to the back of Alastair's gravestone: 'To the beautiful memory of Kenneth Grahame, husband of Elspeth and father of Alastair, who passed the River on the 6th July 1932, leaving childhood and literature through him the more blest for all time.'

After his death, Elspeth worked on, well-liked by her correspondents, and receiving a steady stream of 'pilgrims' to the house. Through Curtis Brown and others she negotiated terms for new editions of *The Wind in the Willows*, and for broadcasting rights (notably to the Wheat and Wool Growers' Union of Western Australia); she approved the manufacture of toys based on the characters, refused to claim royalties for toys made for disabled children and checked (at exemplary speed) the French translation by Mme Eva Léonie Lack (Leo Lack). There was a protracted negotiation with both Roy and Walt Disney over the film rights, in which Elspeth clearly wanted to intervene. In the Bodleian Library archives there is a rather alarmed note to her from Edith Barnes, Curtis Brown's secretary: 'C.B. asked me to tell you that from what he has heard of Disney it would be as well if you didn't write to him, as he doesn't take kindly to suggestions' (19 June 1939).[18] Eventually, the rights were sold to Disney for £500 (around £25,000 in current values). Ironically, as both Elspeth and Curtis Brown felt that

TO
THE BEAUTIFUL MEMORY
OF
KENNETH GRAHAME
HUSBAND OF ELSPETH
AND
FATHER OF ALASTAIR
WHO PASSED THE RIVER
ON THE 6th OF JULY 1932
LEAVING
CHILDHOOD AND LITERATURE
THROUGH HIM
THE MORE BLEST
FOR ALL TIME

THE WIND IN THE WILLOWS

THIS latest addition to Talfourd Toys is a set representing the principal characters in Kenneth Grahame's delightful book. It has been fortunate enough to gain the approval of Mrs. Kenneth Grahame, and of Mr. E. H. Shepard, from whose drawings the figures are taken.

The caravan is made in the form of a box in which the toys can be kept and the figures themselves stand about 4 inches high, have movable limbs and are brightly and attractively coloured.

The characters are as follows :—

Toad	2	0
Toad (as Washerwoman)	2	0
Rat	2	0
Mole	2	0
Badger	2	0
Otter	1	9
Young Portly		6
Hedgehogs		9
Caravan	14	6

MISS ELAINE GRITTON ◆ TALFOURD COTTAGE ◆ REIGATE ◆ SURREY.

ABOVE Elspeth and Curtis Brown were very careful to maintain the quality of any *Wind in the Willows* merchandise after Grahame's death, but also very generous to any deserving causes that wanted to borrow material.

OPPOSITE Passing the river: the grave of Kenneth and Alastair in Holywell Cemetery, Oxford.

The bridge over the Thames between Pangbourne and Whitchurch was, and is, a toll bridge. Elspeth wrote to Curtis Brown: 'Kenneth used to laugh and say that our sole source of income consisted in *not* going over Whitchurch Bridge, which we seldom did, though we constantly stood there.'

only Disney could do artistic justice to the book, the film version, one half of *The Adventures of Ichabod and Mr Toad* (1949) was one of the 'package' films made when Disney's finances, and artistic standards, were both at a low ebb.

And *The Wind in the Willows* went on selling. Kenneth had refused to countenance any adaptations or simplifications, and it is clear that Elspeth felt the same. On 22 March 1934, E.V. Rieu, one of the directors of Methuen, wrote wryly to her:

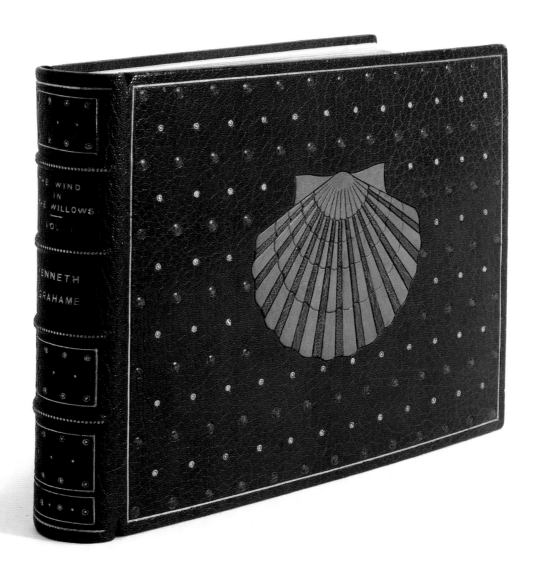

The fine binding of the original manuscript.

The rebellious lower orders are evicted from Toad Hall. Grahame's not-very-PC means of restoring the proper social order, with Shepard brilliantly juggling all the contradictions of scale and the human/animal problem.

You may be interested to know that we have already sold more than 170,000 copies of the *school* edition of 'Wind in the Willows'. I got the figures out a day or so ago in order to provide an effective answer to a school mistress in Canada who wrote to me saying that she thought it would make a nice Reader if we allowed her to re-write it in a simpler style![19]

Despite failing eyesight, Elspeth carried on her wide correspondence until her death in 1946.

Curtis Brown nagged Kenneth for years to write his autobiography but he refused – and yet perhaps he had already written it in the pages of *The Wind in the Willows*. He is the Mole, the rather uptight outsider in the rather louche and aristocratic River Bank society, rather, as in real life, he was a Scot, did not go to university, was not a professional writer, and yet made friends with the likes of 'Q'. In his dreams, he was the Water Rat – the poet of independent means, master of the river, shrewd and knowledgeable – and yet yearning for Italian skies. Part of him was the solid and stolid Badger, insider to great institutions, such as the Bank of England, and impervious to the changes in society. And perhaps most of all, he was Toad – after all, the portrait of Grahame in his greatcoat, dignified moustache, but somewhat startled eyes, could be Toad of the cover of the first edition – Toad whose every instinct is to escape, break the rules, live with the gypsies, drive fast cars and trains, perhaps even flirt with the girl with the buttered toast – or even, perhaps, to take revenge on powerful women.

The Wind in the Willows, that most ambivalent and unclassifiable masterpiece, is, in short, made of Kenneth Grahame.

Notes

1. The Mysteries of
The Wind in the Willows

1 Arnold Bennett, *Books and Persons: Being Comments on a Past Epoch, 1908–1911*, Chatto and Windus, London, 1917, pp. 57–8; Margaret Blount, *Animal Land: The Creatures of Children's Fiction*, Hutchinson, London, 1974, p. 148.
2 Kenneth Grahame, *The Wind in the Willows*, Oxford University Press, Oxford, 2010, p. 93.
3 Ibid., p. 110.
4 Humphrey Carpenter, *Secret Gardens*, Allen and Unwin, London, 1985, p. 168.
5 Grahame, *Willows*, p. 10.
6 Constance Smedley, *Crusaders*, Duckworth, London, 1929, p. 150.

2. The River Banker:
Who was Kenneth Grahame?

1 Curtis Brown, *Contacts*, Cassell, London, 1935, p. 58.
2 Paul Tempest, *The Future of the Bank of England*, Medina Publishing, Newport, Isle of Wight, 2011, p. 52.
3 Oxford, Bodleian Library, MS. Eng. misc. c. 381, fol. 1.
4 *Collected Works of Kenneth Grahame*, ed.
Nigel McMorris, Jason Olson and Inge Williams, Kenneth Grahame Society, Tandragee, Co. Armagh, 2009, p. 395.
5 Patrick Chalmers, *Kenneth Grahame: Life, Letters and Unpublished Work*, Methuen, London, 1933, p. 111.
6 Ibid., p. 51.
7 Oxford, Bodleian Library, MS. Eng. misc. d. 530, fol. 230.
8 'Clarence Onslow', *Amelia Jane's Ambition*, J.W. Arrowsmith, Bristol, 1888, p. 75.
9 Alison Prince, *Kenneth Grahame: An Innocent in the Wild Wood*, Allison and Busby, London, 1994, pp. 226–7.
10 Peter Green, *Kenneth Grahame, 1859–1932: A Study of his Life, Work and Times*, John Murray, London, 1959, p. 205.
11 Oxford, Bodleian Library, MS. Eng. misc. d. 527, fol. 8.
12 Tempest, *Bank*, p. 56.
13 Oxford, Bodleian Library, MS. Eng. misc. e. 481, fol. 1.
14 Oxford, Bodleian Library, MS. Eng. misc. c. 381, fol. 1.
15 Tempest, *Bank*, p. 55.
16 Ibid., pp. 52, 66–70.
17 David J. Holmes, 'Wayfarers All': *Selections from the Kenneth Grahame Collection of David J. Holmes*, Grolier Club, New York, 2008, p. 23.

3. Letters to Mouse:
Drafting the Stories

1 Constance Smedley, *Crusaders*, Duckworth, London, 1929, p. 149.
2 Constance Smedley, *Woman: A Few Shrieks!*, Letchworth, Garden City Press, 1907, facing title page.
3 Oxford, Bodleian Library, MS. Eng. misc. d. 536, fol. 237.
4 Oxford, Bodleian Library, MS. Eng. misc. e. 481, fols 8–9r.
5 Patrick Chalmers, *Kenneth Grahame: Life, Letters and Unpublished Work*, Methuen, London, 1933, p. 121.
6 Elspeth Grahame (ed.), *First Whisper of The Wind in the Willows*, Methuen, London, 1944, p. 2.
7 Smedley, *Crusaders*, p. 151.
8 Kenneth Grahame, *My Dearest Mouse: 'The Wind in the Willows' Letters*, ed. David Gooderson, Pavilion, London, 1988, p. 21.
9 Oxford, Bodleian Library, MS. Eng. misc. e. 482, fols 2–3.
10 Grahame, *Mouse*, p. 64.

4. Messing about in Books:
Building *The Wind in the Willows*

1 Jocelyn Dimbleby, *A Profound Secret*, Black Swan, London, 2004, p. 310.
2 Kenneth Grahame, *The Wind in the Willows*, Oxford University Press, Oxford, 2010, pp. 7, 9.
3 Jerome K. Jerome, *Three Men in a Boat*, Oxford University Press, Oxford, 2008, pp. 13, 58, 59–62.
4 Gordon Stables, *Leaves from the Log of a Gentleman Gypsy in Wayside Camp and Caravan*, Jarrold, London, 1891, pp. 22, 14–15.
5 Grahame, *Willows*, pp. 19, 21.
6 Ibid., pp. 22, 154; Oxford, Bodleian Library, MS. Eng. misc. e. 248, p. 45.
7 E.V. Lucas (ed.), *The Open Road: A Little Book for Wayfarers*, Methuen, London, 1920, p. ix.
8 Ibid., pp. 9, 60, 56, 324, 94–5; *Collected Works of Kenneth Grahame*, ed. Nigel McMorris, Jason Olson and Inge Williams, Kenneth Grahame Society, Tandragee, Co. Armagh, 2009, p. 330.
9 Grahame, *Willows*, p. 77.
10 Ibid., p. 103.

5. Down Stream:
What Happened Afterwards

1 Constance Smedley, *Crusaders*, Duckworth, London, 1929, pp. 152–3.
2 Oxford, Bodleian Library, MS. Eng. misc. d. 530, fol. 204.
3 Curtis Brown, *Contacts*, Cassell, London, 1935, p. 60.
4 Oxford, Bodleian Library, MS. Eng. misc. d. 530, fols 175, 177.
5 Brown, *Contacts*, p. 60.
6 Ibid., pp. 60–1.
7 Oxford, Bodleian Library, MS. Eng. misc. d. 527, fol. 80.
8 Kenneth Grahame (ed.), *The Cambridge Book of Poetry for Children*,

Part 1, Cambridge University Press, Cambridge, 1916, pp. vi–vii.

9 Peter Green, *Kenneth Grahame, 1859–1932: A Study of his Life, Work and Times*, John Murray, London, 1959, p. 338.

10 Oxford, Bodleian Library, MS. Eng. misc. d. 532, fol. 58.

11 Grahame, *Willows*, p. 12.

12 Patrick Chalmers, *Kenneth Grahame: Life, Letters and Unpublished Work*, Methuen, London, 1933, p. 143.

13 Brown, *Contacts*, p. 60.

14 A.A. Milne, *Toad of Toad Hall*, Methuen, London, 1940 [1929], pp. v–vi.

15 Oxford, Bodleian Library, MS. Eng. misc. d. 530, fol. 201.

16 Grahame, *Willows*, p. 17; Roger A. Oakes, *Bibliography of the Works of Kenneth Grahame*, privately printed, 2012, p. 68.

17 Alison Prince, *Kenneth Grahame: An Innocent in the Wild Wood*, Allison and Busby, London, 1994, p. 346.

18 Oxford, Bodleian Library, MS. Eng. misc. e. 379, fol. 162.

19 Oxford, Bodleian Library, MS. Eng. misc. d. 533, fol. 81.

Bibliography

Bennett, A., *Books and Persons: Being Comments on a Past Epoch, 1908–1911*, Chatto and Windus, London, 1917.

Blount, M., *Animal Land: The Creatures of Children's Fiction*, Hutchinson, London, 1974.

Brown, C., *Contacts*, Cassell, London, 1935.

Carpenter, H., *Secret Gardens*, Allen and Unwin, London, 1985.

Chalmers, P., *Kenneth Grahame: Life, Letters and Unpublished Work*, Methuen, London, 1933.

Dimbleby, J., *A Profound Secret*, Black Swan, London, 2004.

Grahame, E., (ed.), *First Whisper of* The Wind in the Willows, Methuen, London, 1944.

Grahame, K., *My Dearest Mouse: 'The Wind in the Willows' Letters*, ed. David Gooderson, Pavilion, London, 1988.

Grahame, K., *The Wind in the Willows*, Oxford University Press, Oxford, 2010.

Grahame, K. (ed.), *The Cambridge Book of Poetry for Children*, Part 1, Cambridge University Press, Cambridge, 1916.

Green, P., *Kenneth Grahame, 1859–1932: A Study of his Life, Work and Times*, John Murray, London, 1959.

Holmes, David J., *'Wayfarers All': Selections from the Kenneth Grahame Collection of David J. Holmes*, The Grolier Club, New York, 2008.

Jerome, Jerome K., *Three Men in a Boat*, Oxford University Press, Oxford, 2008.

Lucas, E.V. (ed.), *The Open Road: A Little Book for Wayfarers*, Methuen, London, 1920.

McMorris, Nigel, Jason Olson and Inge Williams (eds), *Collected Works of Kenneth Grahame*, Kenneth Grahame Society, Tandragee, Co. Armagh, 2009.

Milne, A.A., *Toad of Toad Hall*, Methuen, London, 1940.

Oakes, Roger A., *Bibliography of the Works of Kenneth Grahame*, privately printed, 2012.

'Onslow, C.', *Amelia Jane's Ambition*, J.W. Arrowsmith, Bristol, 1888.

Prince, A., *Kenneth Grahame: An Innocent in the Wild Wood*, Allison and Busby, London, 1994.

Smedley, C., *Crusaders*, Duckworth, London, 1929.

Smedley, C., *Woman: A Few Shrieks!*, Letchworth, Garden City Press, 1907.

Stables, G., *Leaves from the Log of a Gentleman Gypsy in Wayside Camp and Caravan*, Jarrold, London, 1891.

Tempest, P., *The Future of the Bank of England*, Medina Publishing, Newport, Isle of Wight, 2011.

Jan Neele
Wild Wood (1982)

Picture Credits

67 Daimler AG.

68 Oxford, Bodleian Library, G.A. Eng. rivers 4° 27.

69 Oxford, Bodleian Library, MS. Eng. misc. e. 247, fol. 9r.

70 Line Illustration © E.H. Shepard; colouring © 1970, 1971 by E.H. Shepard and Egmont UK Limited. Reproduced with permission of Curtis Brown Group Ltd on behalf of The Shepard Trust. Illustrations provided by Egmont UK Limited and with permission.

71 Private collection.

72 Oxford, Bodleian Library, G.A. Gen. top. 8° 492.

6, 74 Oxford, Bodleian Library, 25325 d.176.

75 Oxford, Bodleian Library, MS. Eng. misc. e. 248, fol. 45.

76 Oxford, Bodleian Library, 2561 e.2052.

78 Line Illustration © E.H. Shepard; colouring © 1970, 1971 by E.H. Shepard and Egmont UK Limited. Reproduced with permission of Curtis Brown Group Ltd on behalf of The Shepard Trust. Illustrations provided by Egmont UK Limited and with permission.

80–1 Oxford, Bodleian Library, 2805 f.176.

85 Oxford, Bodleian Library, MS. Eng. misc. d. 530, fol. 204.

88–9 Oxford, Bodleian Library, MS. Eng. misc. d.530, fols 177, 178.

90 Wikimedia Commons.

92 Oxford, Bodleian Library, X.11.100/ GRAHAME 3, p. 316.

95 Oxford, Bodleian Library, G.A. Eng. rivers 4° 27.

96 Line Illustration © E.H. Shepard; colouring © 1970, 1971 by E.H. Shepard and Egmont UK Limited. Reproduced with permission of Curtis Brown Group Ltd on behalf of The Shepard Trust. Illustrations provided by Egmont UK Limited and with permission.

98 Author.

99 Oxford, Bodleian Library, MS. Eng. misc. c. 720, fol. 61.

100 Shutterstock/Peter Sterling.

101 Oxford, Bodleian Library, MS. Eng. misc. e. 247, 1.

82, 102 Line Illustration © E.H. Shepard; colouring © 1970, 1971 by E.H. Shepard and Egmont UK Limited. Reproduced with permission of Curtis Brown Group Ltd on behalf of The Shepard Trust. Illustrations provided by Egmont UK Limited and with permission.

7, 23, 49, 65, 83 Rackham illustrations: Oxford, Bodleian Library, 25325 d. 176.

Index